cohabitation

For Richard, who does not appear in any of these poems

Kate Bingham
cohabitation

seren

seren
is the book imprint of
Poetry Wales Press Ltd.
First Floor, 2 Wyndham Street
Bridgend, Wales, CF31 1EF

© Kate Bingham, 1998

Cataloguing In Publication Data for this book
is available from the British Library

ISBN:1-85411-215-5

*The publisher acknowledges the financial assistance of the
Arts Council of Wales*

Cover Art: Design from an original photograph by Kate Bingham

Printed by: WBC Book Manufacturers, Bridgend.

Contents

Oxygen

Before you make a start there may be something else
you want to say, perhaps in a professional capacity

or just because it came up recently in a dream,
advertisement, or conversation and seems important.

This is the diminishing return you have to fight all afternoon
because a poem is like a rocket and the difficult bit

falls back to earth with a terrific crash which no one notices
for their ears are beating with drums and blood.

You press your nose to the window. Stones, tracks,
flowering cactus trees shrink into a khaki ocean

and the sea comes up from the horizon like a sunset backwards
as you carve a perfect turn away from the planet

and your bones go light. Unbuckle your belt
and fix yourself to the table now, you are writing effortlessly.

Pay no attention to the clock, the telephone,
the song of ambulances waiting for your imminent return,

and stay in orbit for as long as you have oxygen.
Say what it's like to be so far from home.

Two friends meet for lunch...

Two friends meet for lunch in The Royal Oak
in February. Oxford is ice. I'm nervous,
early. I avoid the barman's eye. Sip coke.

This is the afternoon I loved you first,
clenched throat uttering little carbonated hiccups
of surprise as the door's bell glittered.

Loved instantly your jacket and boots and lips
and hair. Your temperature. Thought: *this is it.*

You nod in my direction and lean at the bar.
Afterwards told me you'd had no idea I felt like that
and joked in bed about my sudden conversion.

Say there's nothing more to it than charisma
but people can never get enough of you. Even the barman,
counting out your change, is passionate.

Still Life

Every day the tulips melt a little,
brave behind their colour, seeping.
The water is clouded with strength.

More cleverly sealed than a spring flower,
you could not survive such a cut.
Your five senses have you covered,

keep you stalking your ambivalence
into the marches of love
and back again. This morning

they look more dead than alive,
improbable heads hold on
to their petals like messengers.

As one they seem to be calling to your
brittle life. A borderland voice,
it longs for you to notice change.

Jealousy

I should never have asked: that sort of question
poisons the heart and answers itself
in the imagination

where teenage hair curls at your shoulder and your
                                          501's are torn.
People are dancing. You walk towards a stranger
and touch her hand. You kiss.

Somewhere, anywhere, she can still taste your saliva
and there's no telling what might happen
next time you meet.

Etudes

I

I woke up
with my fingers wet

but let the spills
and ridges
scab

beneath me
where I'd bled.

II

It was some weeks ago
we shared these sheets.

Sleeping alone
I've kept them so —

covered with promises
of your return,

or reassurances
you were here —

and grown a slovenly
custodian
of love.

III

Washing my hair
you are as much perfectionist
as lover, and keep me sat there —

soap suds on my shoulders
and the bath water
going cold.

IV

My half of the bed is narrower than yours
and wrinkled with care
because the sheet will only tuck
beneath the mattress one side at a time
and this week it's your turn.

V

Let me dip my finger
in the egg-yolk of your ear;

it is eighteen days
and now my nails are long enough.

The greenhouse
harbours flies

but pollen from the tongues of lilies
is not a lovelier colour

than those flakes of wax
I yearn to print.

VI

When you are away
I sleep with cushions and books
and two hot water bottles

which I worry will burst,
leaking rubbery piss into the mattress.
I keep my underwear on

and dream of other men. Wake up
pleased to have turned them down
before it was too late.

Often the duvet will have slipped
from your side of the bed,
leaving the naked sheet smooth.

The weight of it presses me tight
against the edge. I am disorientated,
and eat cereal three times a day.

Things I Learned at University

How to bike on cobblestones and where to signal right.
How to walk through doors held open by Old Etonians
and not scowl. How to make myself invisible in seminars
by staring at the table. How to tell Victorian Gothic
                                             from Medieval.
How to eat a Mars bar in the Bodleian. When to agree
with everything in theory. How to cultivate a taste for sherry.

Where to bike on the pavement after dark. How to sabotage
                                                 a hunt.
When to sunbathe topless in the Deer Park. When to punt.
How to hitch a lift and when to walk and where to run.
When not to address my tutors formally. How to laugh at
                                             Latin puns
and when to keep quiet and preserve my integrity.
How to celebrate an essay crisis. When to sleep through
                                             fire alarms.

How to bike no-handed, how to slip a condom on with one.
When to smoke a joint and when to swig champagne.
When to pool a tip and how to pull a pint. A bit of history.
When to listen to friends and whether to take them seriously.
At the same time how to scorn tradition and enjoy it.
How to live like a king, quite happily, in debt.

Castellan

Baileys were comparatively intractable —

the curvilinear plan
could be turned into some sort of polygon

and a single tower built upon it
or a ring.

As money became available
outer defences,

to accommodate the less essential parts
or simply to delay,

sealed off penetration by retrenchment —

a narrow corridor,

every inch within stone-throwing range
of the battlements.

February

There is a new breeze in the flat
and somewhere a door swings gently,
knocking its stiff tongue against the frame.
Soft, anonymous fibres inch across the floor
and simply because there have been colder days
it feels like spring.

Line Drawings

I went about Mexico without a camera
and marvelled like an old man
wheeled into the garden one last time,
photographing the pyramids with my hands.

So as to attract more visitors the guides
put everything down to human sacrifice.
In afternoon rain the jungle gleamed,
leaves flickered like notation under the weight
of such huge warm drops and Palenque held still.

You spoke of instinct as if it were the same as memory,
as if my sense of direction were a map
passed down like some inherited gene or chip
and one day I'd go somewhere no ancestor of mine
had ever been and find myself quite suddenly lost.

My great-great-grandfather built railways
and took his daughter around the world.

In order that they should be the first to steam
                              into Havana
arm-chairs were lashed to the front
of the locomotive. A sketch in her journal
shows four shoes dangling, mid-air, above the tracks
and both heads down, watching the sleepers blur.

I thought of them sailing to Veracruz across the Gulf,
not very many miles from here.

Caught

Grandpa, that story you tell
about the war, I read it
in an obituary last week.

"British pilot had
captured German U-boat,
a singular feat," it said.

Face to Face

My mother claims she could tell when I was ill,
even before I felt it — something unfamiliar in the smell
of my breath would jar, like a wrong note.

Animals scent fear and this can stimulate
the natural dominance of one species over another.
Mum could identify the fragrance of dishonesty,

half-truths, white lies. Now we communicate in other ways,
by post, long distance telephone, and this is how relationships
turn sour. Intuition fades, language takes over.

Chintz

Granny, I loved the material
which covered the four-piece suite
you chose for your retirement.

You may have scolded me
for clambering over the sofa in my out-door shoes
and made me take them off to watch your colour TV

but the sound I could get
scraping my fingernails down the back
of Grandpa's chair sent shivers up my spine.

The summer I turned sixteen
it seemed unusual
to be inking in

the faded red, threadbare
between white cabbage roses, big as faces,
with a ball-point pen.

Playtime, with Boys

I have been waiting for Wednesday, when we are lions
holding hands across a field of wildebeest.

I have thought of it with every time a little more
excitement, I have made a plan.

The enemy will chant their songs as we
blow kisses, single out our prey

having, for half an hour, the most exhilaration
we are allowed all week.

Wednesday is a football I can kick intelligently,
whamming the goal like a star.

All the boys will have to admit I'm good, I'm playing well,
and all the boys I love will wish they hadn't

said the things they said to me since last Wednesday,
when hordes of warriors

poured out of the separate playground and I was Hippolyta
and the teachers kept to their corners,

telling themselves this was just an ordinary gang of children
letting off steam.

Sex

When I came home from school and told my mother
I was surprised she had even heard
of anything so disgusting.

She sat me in the kitchen and explained that fucking
was the closest a man and a woman could get
to wanting the same thing at the same time
and one day, when I was older, I would understand
that this was love.

Physics

Two messages appeared on the notice-board
when Brezhnev died,

one warning that the future of world peace
hung in the balance.

If every human being jumped simultaneously,
the other asserted,
the earth would swing out of orbit.

To avoid the possibility of such a huge coincidence
our whole class
promised never to leap needlessly again.

Stuck, this afternoon, for something more to say to the 11
about medieval coins

I tell them the ice in the gas meter trick.
It boosts my popularity.

Freebies

There must be dozens of them in the flat,
lurking in pencil cases, skulking with rubber bands
and pots of dried-up Tippex in the darkest corners
of deep drawers.

Boglins I didn't have the heart to throw away.
Skeletron. The snouty-nosed Snaffle, an elaborate
                                            paper clip.
Zip and Zap the Pop-Munchers and Smiley, best of all,
a pea-green crocodile whose tail wraps round the end
                                            of a pen,
making it impossible to write.

Last year, during exams, I found him hiding
in my coat pocket, a lucky mascot, and this morning
bring him to school to bribe my class. First one, I say,
to finish the comprehension gets this prize.

They laugh. They seem to like the thought of Miss
eating Frosties for breakfast.

Nits

Lobby your ministers to sign the multilateral declaration NOW,
and help exterminate headlice in just forty-two days
by keeping your hair as greasy as you can. People, throw away
those fine tooth combs and feel our planet relax
as the itching stops.

Shampoo sales will slump, short-term, and the manufacturers
of Prioderm, of course, go out of business. Factories
may close,
redundancies produce despair and crime waves in our cities,
but the net effect on the economy will be minimal.

Let animal rights campaigners demonstrate in Hyde Park
objecting to the systematic annihilation of one species by another
and let Jeremy Paxman interview a panel of scientists
on insect contributions to the search for a cure for cancer.

Lawyers and historians will urge the public to resist
a dangerous extension of political power, arguing that
parliament has no competence to legislate on personal hygiene,
a fundamental human right, but we will stand firm.

There is little sympathy for the parasites
and popular opinion lies with the government.

The View

I am pointing at the horizon.
"Look over there: York Minster," I say,
as if I were my mother. "Can't you see?"
This is as far north as you have ever been.

You peer at thirteen miles of ripening farmland,
then put your glasses on. You close one eye.
Squinting along my index finger,
square your cool left cheek against my right.

Three power stations and an office block appear.
In front of them, two tall trees,
a cottage with a dog — a puppy, you think —
in the garden. A golden retriever.

Somebody out of sight shouts "fetch!"
and the idiot puppy bounds
in the opposite direction, but still
you tell me, no, you cannot see the Minster.

I look at the view. I wonder
where it can have gone. I pick a flower.
"Vetch, related to sweet-pea" I say,
as if I were my father.

Evensong

Warm June, the land soft green, and bird-song: dusk
                                                    is falling.
The mermaid rose endeavours to prolong late afternoon,
and honeysuckle to delay the evening.
The garden holds its breath as if to stay the rising moon.

Tangled grasses in the field suspend the hour.
In the orchard boughs try not to bend; the daisies wait.
Dew wells on the lawn and shadows lean. But still the
                                                    flowers
of marsh and hedgerow hesitate.

Only the stream will disappear at twilight.
As though unable to withstand the imminence
of midsummer darkness it rushes into the night
too quick for touch to catch or sense.

Love

There were so many flies we spoke in sign language
and wore long socks and sun-glasses for protection.

Just thinking of them as eggs or creamy worms
writhing, unseen, in the flower heads
could make you sick,

but it was a kind of torture, with the grasses deep
and the air so soft,
not to go out into the haze.

A kind of ecstasy to risk bare skin
in the profusion.

A Lover's Guide

You are wearing that secretive mysterious expression,
the one which makes me laugh like I used to laugh
when I was a little girl about to be tickled
(raise an eyebrow and my bladder will explode),

bending to unplug the television, patiently
untangling its grimy lead. You heave and bundle it
through the door as if it were a woman, biting and
                                            scratching
all the way to the barn, and you a cowboy.

You come back, silently, to take the video too and now
                                            I follow
along the corridor, upstairs. I wait outside our door
and run into the bathroom when it opens,
hiding behind the shower curtain, getting my feet wet.

You call my name. I will not come. You will not fetch me.
The hysteria dies down and I give in to curiosity.
We lie naked in bed with our glasses on and giggle
at the screen. Three million lovers can't be wrong.

Radio

The tortoise won because the hare
ran out of energy.

Frequency equals
number of steps to cross the floor
divided by two.

High winds. Empty words.
Especially in space, where there's no friction.

Don't talk to me about Glen Gould.

Each station emits its own distinctive scent,
just one of which will prove irresistible
to the attentive radio. They mate.

How would *you* dance to
"Every little thing she does is magic"?

Fruit

Possessing the ability to cure colds.
Eaten by Queen Victoria.
Which smells like rotting flesh.
Containing twenty-three seeds or more.

Stepped into the carpet.
And nut.
Suitable for wedding cake.
Alive with maggots.

Commonly mistaken for a vegetable.
With yellow skin.
Painted by Vermeer.
Green.

From America.
Remembered in my grandfather's will.
Grown less than six feet from ground level.
Which will roll.

Entertainment

After the negotiations — when we are all
left alone together, seated in accordance,
a willing periphery — must come the action.

So here is the ringmaster, top hat and whip
tipped jaunty with the rhetoric of control,
and here is the clown.

Decorated animals trot round and round
beneath the tightrope-walker as she swings
her hips and winks her sequins in our open eye

though you notice fresh sawdust has been scattered
since yesterday's unfortunate circumstance.
That in-take of breath as the disconnected net

met the ground and the stunts really began,
today is ours to release after her first short steps.
Held in like this we are easy anthropology,
a closed crowd loving it.

Lido

Passers-by forgot themselves
and stood around the edge of a mended hole
watching it turn back into a swimming pool.

For the first few hours we could see two trickles
of water dribbling from the vents at the shallow end,
winding like rivulets across a turquoise estuary.

Later the depth welled upward like a mystery
and huge invisible fish swerved this way and that,
dimpling the glassy surface.

Clouds broke up and soon the open sky
was blue blue blue like a drink of summer,
nearly, but not quite ready yet, to sip.

Walking to Africa

Dolphins rescued us from the island.
Enchanted by their dance
we waded up to our thighs in the Mediterranean

further and further from the shore
until even the mountain horns disappeared
behind the curve of the earth.

It was hard to guess their number.
Sunlight glittered on the smoky-blue water
and dark spots swam across the horizon.

Slowly our tired legs grew strong,
our bodies felt lighter.
No one said a word

but when the sun went down and we rested
you touched me, moving your lips.
Then the dolphins leapt

and we stood up again, dripping fire. We walked on.
And the stars came out above us
and below us the plankton.

Yellow Moon

We should have sex: a tropical night like this
and both of us unable to sleep.

Quicker than it takes two paracetamol
to soothe the heart into a stupor we could fall in love again.

Flick on the radio, lie back swooning as the first fat drops
of the rainy season slap the pavement, turn to steam.

It's warm enough to make the dead and buried sweat.
Live water-birds sleep in the duvet

shifting their body-weight, intimately,
prodding my tits and belly

with their delicate wet feet.
They fidget, wake up looking for fleas, take fright.

Keep away from me, you say, stop making me sticky.
Touch, and we might never separate.

Meditation

Why do so many cars drive past my window this morning?
On Sundays people are supposed to lie late in bed,
go nowhere and do nothing.

More brilliant than the window pane and bluer
than the drawn lace curtain let it seem, the sky unbends.
I'd guess the cars were headed for the sea,

if it were not so far. Some people can tell one kind of engine
from another just by listening, the same way others
know the size and hollowness of waves,

their colour, ocean, temperature.
The sound of cars is sighs intensified. An unsteady wind.
Waves collapsing one by one against the sand.

The heavy, round stones beyond the water's reach
are moments of silence in between. They lie late in the sun,
go nowhere and do nothing.

August

August is a heap of peach skins
at the side of your plate.
Intricate pits, licked clean,
and off-cuts where touches
crushed the sweet white flesh.

Dressed in softest summer fur
my fingers will long be sticky
with the memory of scent and spit.

Our leavings bleach
and hover-flies nudge your ear.

Because my mother and father...

Because my mother and father
hurt each other
I will abandon you

sooner or later
somebody will learn
from the experience

that imitation
has nothing to do
with flattery.

De Beers

At first it's microscopic. A bubble in a bubble
in a stoppered bottle of champagne, it incubates.

It carries on a wind of violins, hooks into her finger like
                                        a thorn,
a wart seed chewing through layer after layer of skin.

Steadily it works itself to the very bone and grows
as fat and white as a blister, harder than a stone.

It ladders her tights and gets infected, snagging hair and coats
as she brushes up against them on the tube, in restaurants.

She keeps her fist in her pocket, learns to shop with gloves.
She gets verruca acid on prescription and a packet of
                                        elastoplast

which curls in the bath and peels off soggy polos of dead flesh
to give the parasite a more pronounced appearance.

Steadily she grows accustomed to its face. She cleans it
with a cotton-wool bud dipped in liquid nitrogen.

It starts to gleam. And now she looks at it all the time,
twisting her hand this way and that in the sunlight,
                                        like a fiancée.

Beaujolais

Still drunk at midnight we find a small French restaurant,
demand to eat frogs' legs, snails and *tarte tatin*.
We order more wine, more cigarettes from the machine
and laugh too much. Sarah laughs quietly as well,
at something we're not meant to know about yet,
but there it is in her breasts, her cup of sugary camomile,
curled up fluttering in the hollow of her throat,
not quite asleep. Vinegar rings the red-check table-cloth,
there's ash in the cracks between the demerara cubes,
a Michaelmas daisy in a vase. We laugh and laugh
because it's Friday and everything seems hilarious
and suddenly this is what we should be frightened of.
The music finishes. Tomorrow comes. We cluster
at the foot of the stair and wait for taxis, for the thought of it
to pass.

Out Shooting

Muddy dogs quarter the marsh
and the snipe blow cover,
leaping into cartwheels like a spray of knives.
You squeeze the trigger.

Little birds are easier to down.
The pellets fly out in a kind of triangle
and it only takes one to splinter a wing.
I mark exactly where it fell

and now the snipe is flapping and kicking
on the grass, frantic with pain.
I know I wanted you to fire. The palm of my hand
still hurts where my nails dug in.

Senate House

Terrazzo after dusty linoleum
and book upon book upon book.
Porcelain. An actual echo.

So different it could be another world
if it weren't for the views over Russell Square
and through the drizzle to St Paul's.

Some afternoons I just come here to rest
in the fresh grey rain-light
and think

how I would love to smoke
a long white cigarette
leaning out of that wide open window.

Across the wastes...

Across the wastes
I run

towards the river —

frost has untraced
the lines,

the pitches have become
Siberia,

my face
a second sun.

Questionnaire

Never so anxious I can hardly stand it,
or afraid to show my violence
livid upon the task at hand.

Sleeping as well as usual,
I remember what I ought no trouble:
cups of tea, postcards —

I haven't experienced a major trauma.
People I know see clearly
the consequences of enjoyment.

With no special effort
most of the things I want I am achieving,
somewhat differently;

there is nobody to ring.
Understand that I have never lost
anything dear to me, nor any one.

Bauble

The Silk Cut ad in this week's copy of *Time Out*
entertainment guide for London.

Page 47 of the *A to Z Road Atlas of Great Britain*,
Lampeter, where I have never been.

The back of a book of poetry with excerpts
from a good review. The backs of other books,

the side-board, chess-board, chopping board —
so many surfaces I can't make out the shape

of the space I'm meant to be working in, or count
its dimensions. Paper the cracks,

attach it to a length of red embroidery thread
and hang from the anglepoise

above the table where I write and stare at my hands.
Wiped clean, the grain in the wood could be

the contours of some Cambrian mountain,
the bauble an imaginary sun.

The Vacancy

Blame it on what I like,
I will still need to be young and dynamic

whatever the situation.
Crowded platform, empty underground station.

Patience is running out.
My only qualification hurts my feet.

The train approaching is a train
that's headed in approximately the right direction.

Put yourself in my position: seventeen applicants
push their way into a compartment

already fat with vacancies
already taken, permanent trouser creases,

swivel chairs on wheels,
marble corridors with their own high heels,

satisfied requirements and answered advertisements,
years and years and years of experience

crammed into the same dark filing cabinet drawer.
Do you understand me yet?

It could be anybody's guts
I'm staring through. It could be yours.

Connoisseur

Never to feel the cold,
slipping out into the Atlantic

just to appreciate
the texture of another sea

the way a salmon might
long to be slung into water from

one particular loch,
completely immersed in delight,

and unaffected by
the possibility of ice.

Diversion

There are no landmarks in the middle of the night
but none of this would have happened
if you'd been with me in the car.
You would have picked a different route,
gone left at the roundabout, not right.
You would have made me read the map,
pull over, get out and ask a passer-by.
You would have opened the sunshine roof,
no matter how cold it was, and driven by the stars.
But this is my journey and I am leaving you behind.
The passer-by shoulders into an all-night chippy.
I follow a bus the wrong way down Southampton Street.

After Ovid

"Lie in that bath much longer and you'll dissolve
or change into some new species of aquatic mammal
with shrivelled arms for fins and thorny skin."
You tried to smile. You pointed to the membrane
concertinaed between your toes.
I had to carry you downstairs in sailcloth
padded with damp towels like a bunch of flowers.
Volunteers followed with watering cans
and sponges, the way they care for stranded whales.
There were photographs in the newspaper.
The BBC arrived in time to film our last good-bye
and millions of viewers wrote in to say
how moved they were when I lay with you
on the tow-path and held your flipper.
I launched a nation-wide appeal
to clean up the canal and had it stocked
with Dublin Bay Prawns and Dover Sole.
The Anglers' Club had to go and fish elsewhere.
I watched the same spot every day for a year,
thinking you might swim by and wave or show
some sign of affection. I would have loved
to see you leap like a dolphin. Later I just wanted
to know you had survived the transformation
and found myself unlocking the bathroom door
in search of an answer. Algae floated
in ancient puddles on the floor. I took off my clothes,
stepped into your cold water and lay down.
Dust and pubic hair dragged at the meniscus.
My fingers creased. The days turned into weeks
and months, and I gave up believing in evolution.

Vision Two

36 x 65 in (99 x 165 cm.)

The sky is grey, as in so many of the earlier paintings,
but bright, its hundred thousand
snow-flakes marked in pencil after the pigment dried.
Stand to one side and notice the way they vanish
as the surface of the picture catches the light.

The motorway, depicted here in traditional flat white
cuts up from the very frame to dominate
the foreground, ruthlessly unbalancing Taylor's composition,
and a signpost, centre right, the frail blue rectangle,
tells us the road heads west.

Every lane is traffic jammed. Motorcars stand bumper-to-
                                                    bumper,
up to their hub-caps in snow.
Careful investigation has shown that Taylor painted these
first in colour, subsequently covering the bodywork
with layer upon layer of chalk, for authenticity.

Most of the engines have run out of fuel but, here
                                          and there,
thick yellow clouds of exhaust deepen the fog.
In one car a woman and a man are wrestling on the
                                          passenger seat.
Across the central reservation, upper left, cigarettes and sweets
                                          change hands.

Crib

High winds demolished the cowshed late on Christmas Eve
leaving a gap in the horizon, half a wall, the cherry tree
bent double and four or five tons of solid shit.

Its falling down was a slow accomplished test of gravity,
timbers shifting inch by inch as decades flashed past,
regimes tumbled and dynasties collapsed.

The animals low and shiver in a distant corner of their field,
trampling the phone-line so now the receiver dings randomly
and whispers nonsense in your ear. Cars arrive sideways.

Old aunts cluster like parsnips and sprouts in the kitchen,
rattling ice-cream cartons heavy with spare ancestral cutlery.
Uncles roll their Sunday sleeves and circle the mire,

cigarettes cupped, arms folded, shaking their heads
at father and me. We slip and clamber across the wreckage,
hauling off earthy beams in the rain.

Wax Flowers

A poet steps into the light and waits
for the applause to stop. Two plastic chairs
and a Turkish rug have been assembled on the platform
but he knows he isn't meant to sit.

He knows he isn't meant to turn his back on the audience
and that he must speak slowly, more slowly
than one would think, and offer anecdotes
or explanations for the literary bits.

He has decided to avoid all poems containing language
of a sexually explicit or otherwise offensive nature
and is secretly disappointed to find that this
rules out so little of his work.

Mineral water sloshes from his polystyrene cup.
He presses it into the carpet with his foot,
and as he opens his latest collection
several torn-off scraps of paper flutter out.

"The first line of this poem isn't true," he mumbles.
"The house was actually in Yorkshire but Yorkshire
didn't scan so I changed it to Kent..."
He has found his place, and folded the paperback

in half, the wrong way, breaking its slender spine.
He reads. He goes down well. During the interval
he takes a mug of cheap Rioja and regrets
not having brought more books to sell.

Cromwell Road

An elderly man, bow-legged, but quite respectable
in overcoat and cap and slip-on shoes
three different shades of beige, half-shuffles
half-staggers along the pavement slowly,
(he is too proud to use his stick) in my direction.

His hair, he has hair, also in beige, is neat
and seems to have been trimmed recently.
Possibly he has had it dyed to match his outfit.
If so, there is no perfect match. That same visit
the barber also clipped his nostril hairs.

His eyebrows, however, have been left to silver.
They are overgrown, perhaps a lover once admired
their bushiness. Yes, he is handsome.
Thirty or twenty years ago he would not have looked at me
the way he looks at me now. He wants to ask a favour.

On his left lapel there sits a large white sticker with
"New Hampshire Tours to the Old World"
printed in royal blue capitals across the top.
Beneath it "Walter Perator", in felt-tip pen.
He is American and he has lost his wife and his hotel.

I offer him my arm. I tell him everything will be all right
and take him home.

How to Play

Think of a number — any — from one to forty-nine
and take away the common denominator of the dates of birth
of all your father's living relatives, including your own.
Divide by politics and religion and a piece of arable
with planning permission somewhere outside Northallerton,
round up to the nearest motorway junction
and subtract a fraction of the price you could have got.
Remainder everyone and everything you cared about
and halve your debt. Multiply the cost of living
where the jobs are by your quarterly telephone bill
and take away the square root of the bus route home,
the sum of last month's income tax and NI contributions.
Square the company's responsibility towards its shareholders,
factorial your hours. Calculate average one night stands
per annum as a function of loss to the power of love,
the difference between a round of drinks and the little black
stretchy number with the sweet-heart neck you wear
with nothing underneath but perfume and deodorant.
Multiply by fifty-two Saturdays a year and dance all night
to the tune of twenty-four million pounds. Divide by one.

Home Sweet Home

I need a chocolate bar I can live with,
nothing too big, a red-brick biscuit base, perhaps,
south-facing, on a quiet, tree-lined residential street
where parking late at night won't be a problem.

Nothing too crumbly either. I don't want
to be sweeping up bits of cornice all weekend
and pestering the surveyor with each new crack
in the milky bar matt emulsion shell.

It's got to be the sort of place I can forget about,
with cocoa solids minimum 65 per cent
and nougat foundations limed with soya lecithin
cement and bourneville guttering

no matter what the cost because you can't price
peace of mind and that means no original features,
nothing too fancy, nothing architect-designed.
There's only me, I know exactly what I'm looking for,

not space so much as surface area, a honey-comb interior,
with wafer walls and butterscotch parquet
leading from room to room, each mouthful lighter,
sweeter than the one before and breathed, not tasted,

like a puff of icing sugar. Coming home
will be a hit, a score. I'll drop my hand-bag in the hall,
tie back my hair, lie down and lick the floor.

In Passing

I would like to be a woman in a poem.
Something by Milosz, perhaps, or Brodsky,
mentioned at the end of a stanza
almost casually —

the flare of a skirt, bright red,
suspended and still vanishing round the corner
of a certain derelict building
in the poet's home town.

A laugh with music in it — bells! —
that sounds like the laugh of somebody else
the poet once knew, when he was younger.
Ah, but she never came to America.

Lemon and jasmine. Menthol cigarettes.
I won't mind that the poet
only notices what he has already remembered,
that the poem only hints.

Reading it you wouldn't be able to say
exactly who he saw,
but only that it was a woman
who reminded you of me.

November

Beads of transparent yellow jelly —
more of them each week, in delicate clusters —
form at the bottom of the window pane.
Some species of mould, I suspect,
between the glass and the metal frame.

Mornings we can't see through
for condensation. The city shimmers
and streams with indoor rain —
our every breath accounted for, distilled.
We sleep without the radiator on and dress in bed.

Acknowledgements

I am grateful to the editors of the following magazines in which some of these poems first appeared: *Poetry Wales, The North, Pennine Platform, The Rialto, Oxford Poetry.*

I would also like to thank the Society of Authors and the judges of the 1996 Eric Gregory Awards.

'Castellan' was inspired by a passage from *The Castle in England* and Wales by D.J. Cathcart King.